HISTORY OF FUN STUFF

The Scoop on Ice Cream!

by Bonnie Williams
illustrated by Scott Burroughs

Ready-to-Read

Simon Spotlight

New York   London   Toronto   Sydney   New Delhi

SIMON SPOTLIGHT

An imprint of Simon & Schuster Children's Publishing Division
1230 Avenue of the Americas, New York, New York 10020
This Simon Spotlight edition August 2014
For information about special discounts for bulk purchases,
please contact Simon & Schuster Special Sales at 1-866-506-1949 or
business@simonandschuster.com.
The Simon & Schuster Speakers Bureau can bring authors to your live event.
For more information or to book an event contact the Simon & Schuster Speakers Bureau at
1-866-248-3049 or visit our website at www.simonspeakers.com.
Manufactured in the United States of America 0614 LAK
2 4 6 8 10 9 7 5 3 1
Library of Congress Cataloging-in-Publication Data
Williams, Bonnie.
The scoop on ice cream / by Bonnie Williams ; illustrated by Scott Burroughs. — First edition.
pages cm. — (Ready-to-read. Level 3) (History of fun stuff)
Summary: "Chill out with the fascinating history behind ice cream, the first in a fact-tastic Level 3
Ready-to-Read nonfiction series about the history of fun stuff! Did you know that immigrants to
Ellis Island were served ice cream as part of their first meal in America? Or that George Washington
spent more than $200 on ice cream during the summer of 1790? Learn all about the cool history of
everyone's favorite frozen treat in this fun, fact-filled Level 3 reader. A special section at the back of
the book includes relevant info on subjects like geography and science, and there's even a fun quiz so
you can test yourself to see what you've learned!"— Provided by publisher.
ISBN 978-1-4814-0981-0 (paperback) — ISBN 978-1-4814-0982-7 (hardcover) — ISBN 978-1-4814-0983-4 (eBook)
1. Ice cream, ices, etc.—History—Juvenile literature. I. Burroughs, Scott, illustrator. II. Title.
TX795.W715 2014
641.86'2—dc23
2013044729

CONTENTS

CHAPTER 1
The Origins of Ice Cream

You know lots of things about ice cream, right? You know it's delicious, and you know your favorite flavor. You also know that ice cream comes in cups or cones and that you eat it with a spoon or just lick it right off the scoop. But what do you know about the history of ice cream? Do you know who invented it and when? Or which United States presidents loved ice cream?

Today if you have a hankering for ice cream, it is easy enough to find some—you just buy it from the supermarket or go to your favorite ice-cream parlor and order a scoop (or two!).

But did you know it wasn't always so easy to satisfy your craving? And do you know where those scoops came from or how they were made? That's where this book comes in. By the time you finish reading this book, you will know the answers to these questions and many more. You will be a History of Fun Stuff Expert on ice cream!

The history of ice cream is not an easy one to piece together. Sometimes it seems about as clear as a bowl of ice-cream soup, and just as messy! What historians do know for sure is that frozen treats have been enjoyed for at least two thousand years.

ICE CREAM

In ancient times, snow and ice were combined with flavors like honey, fruit, and juice. Nero, a Roman emperor who ruled ancient Italy from the year 54 to the year 68, would make his slaves run up high into the mountains for ice.

When the slaves returned, they added fruit and juice to the ice to make something we'd recognize today as a slushie or Italian ice.

The Chinese were probably the first to mix ice and snow with milk, making a creamy dish that more closely resembles the ice cream we know and love today. There is a record of frozen dairy treats made of milk, flour, and camphor as far back as the Tang Dynasty that began in the year 618 and ended in 907. Camphor is a substance that comes from the camphor tree. It has a very strong smell. Today camphor is used in mothballs, gels to help with colds, and insect repellent. Just don't eat any of those!

It took centuries for ice cream to make its way from China to Europe. There are many legends about how it did so. One of the most famous ones involves a man you may have already heard of named Marco Polo. In the 1200s, he traveled from Italy to China. Some say that he returned with recipes for ice cream, but there is no

evidence to support this. Regardless, by the 1600s, ice cream was enjoyed throughout Europe, and in the later half of the century, it was being served at the royal court of England. Not long after this, ice cream arrived in the American colonies.

CHAPTER 2
Almost Modern History

Ice cream has been a part of the American way of life since the very beginning, even before the Declaration of Independence was signed in 1776. When the states were still colonies of England, the well-to-do would serve ice cream at parties and other events.

One night in 1744, the governor of the Maryland colony served ice cream after dinner. We know about this because one of his guests was so amazed by the dessert that he wrote about it in a letter. This is the oldest record of ice cream in the Americas.

Our founding fathers and mothers had a real sweet tooth for ice cream too. In 1790, George Washington was a year into being the first president of the United States. That summer, he and his wife, Martha, spent $200 on ice cream. That's a lot of money, but it's even more when you think about how much that would be worth today.

Unfortunately, it's hard to calculate the value of money from that far back, but we do know that as little as one hundred years ago, $200 was worth more than $4,700! How much ice cream do you think you could buy with that much money?

Another founding father and the third president of the United States, Thomas Jefferson, is known for having done many things. He wrote the Declaration of Independence and started his own university, the University of Virginia. But did you know that he also loved ice cream? He kept a recipe for vanilla ice cream written in his own handwriting.

He discovered this recipe in France, where he was an ambassador before he became the American president. When he returned to the United States, he would often serve ice cream at his parties. If you had been seated at Thomas Jefferson's table, there is a good chance you would have eaten ice cream based on this recipe.

ICE-CREAM RECIPE

Until the mid-1800s, making ice cream was hard work that took hours to be done by hand. Then, in 1843, a woman named Nancy Johnson patented the first ice-cream maker that made the work a bit easier. Here's how her machine worked:

- US PATENT -

You'd start with two cans, one smaller, one larger. In the smaller can, you would add your basic ice-cream ingredients like milk, sugar, and flavoring. Then you would add ice and salt to the larger can and fit the smaller can inside.

Next you'd use a crank to churn the ingredients in the smaller can. This made the mixture smooth and creamy, while the ice in the larger can simultaneously froze it.

After about twenty to forty-five minutes of cranking, you could enjoy your ice cream.

Sound like fun? If you want to make ice cream the old-fashioned way, there are companies that still sell ice-cream makers based on Nancy Johnson's original design.

Because of Nancy Johnson's invention, more people were able to experience the joy of eating ice cream. Another turning point came a few years later, in 1851, when a man named Jacob Fussell opened the first ice-cream factory. As you might expect, his business boomed, and he soon opened up other factories. For the first time in its long history, ice cream was being manufactured on a large scale. To this day, Jacob Fussell is known as the father of the ice-cream industry.

FATHER OF THE
ICE-CREAM INDUSTRY

JACOB FUSSELL

CHAPTER 3
The Scoop on Scoops—
Cones, Sundaes, and More!

With ice cream available to everyone, the stage was now set for classic ice-cream dishes to take shape. And speaking of taking shape, you might not believe it, but there was a time when the ice-cream cone didn't exist. It's hard to pinpoint exactly who invented the cone.

The best evidence shows that there were a number of people who independently came up with the idea of eating ice cream out of edible cones. However, cones weren't popular until the St. Louis World's Fair in 1904 where many vendors sold them. After that, there was no turning back. The ice-cream cone was here to stay!

What about ice-cream sundaes? Like the invention of the ice-cream cone, the origin of the ice-cream sundae is up for debate. Some believe that it was invented in 1881 in Two Rivers, Wisconsin, when chocolate sauce was drizzled on top of scoops of ice cream.

Others say it was 1892, in Ithaca, New York, when cherry syrup and a cherry were added to a dish of ice cream. In both stories, the dish was named after the day, Sunday, on which it was either invented or often served. Today there's a friendly rivalry between Ithaca and Two Rivers about the true birthplace of the sundae.

Last but not least, what about ice-cream novelties? No frozen section of a grocery store would be complete without ice-cream sandwiches, pops, and bars. How and when did they come about? The first ice-cream novelty was vanilla ice cream covered in a chocolate shell, known as an Eskimo Pie.

It was invented in 1920 by a high school teacher in Iowa who also sold ice cream. He got inspired by an eight-year-old customer who couldn't decide between buying a chocolate bar or ice cream. Since both are delicious, the teacher came up with a way of combining them!

CHAPTER 4
Ice Cream Today

As you know, you can find ice cream everywhere these days. It is so much a part of our culture that when immigrants arrived on Ellis Island in the early 1900s, they were served ice cream. Today almost ten percent of milk production in the United States goes into the manufacturing of ice cream in every flavor and type imaginable. The ice-cream industry makes a profit of ten billion dollars every year!

ICE-CREAM FACTORY

How does the ice-cream industry make so much money? It's because Americans love ice cream! The average American eats about eighty cups of ice cream every year. Depending on the size of your scoop, that's two to four scoops every four and a half days!

Ice cream has been so popular that in 1984, Ronald Reagan, the fortieth president of the United States, named July as National Ice-Cream Month. Every year, the official National Ice-Cream Day is the third Sunday of July.

\-JULY 1984\-						
SUNDAY	MONDAY	TUESDAY	WEDNESDAY	THURSDAY	FRIDAY	SATURDAY
1	2	3	4	5	6	7
8	9	10	11	12	13	14
15	16	17	18	19	20	21
22	23	24	25	26		28
29	30	31				

Do you know what the most popular
flavor of ice cream is in the United States?

The answer probably won't surprise you. It's vanilla, followed by chocolate. Combined, they make up about fifty percent of ice-cream sales. Which of those two flavors do you prefer? Do you have another favorite flavor? Do you know which flavor is your best friend's favorite?

As you can probably imagine, ice cream isn't just popular in the United States. People in other countries love ice cream too. But what are some favorite flavors around the world? In Japan, there's an ice-cream flavor made with squid ink.

FISH EGG ICE CREAM

GARLIC ICE CR

SQUID INK ICE CREAM

And you can find ice cream topped with caviar, also known as fish eggs, in France. But not to be outdone, the United States also makes its share of unique flavors. You can find pizza-flavored ice cream, bacon-flavored ice cream, and even garlic-flavored ice cream! Would you eat any of these flavors? Can you think of other flavors you've never heard of but would be willing to try?

BACON ICE CREAM

PIZZA ICE CREAM

EXPERT

HISTORY
OF FUN STUFF
EXPERT
ON
ICE
CREAM

Congratulations! You've come to the end of this book. You are now an official History of Fun Stuff Expert on ice cream. Go ahead and impress your friends and family with all the cool things you know about the world's coolest treat. And the next time you take a lick off your scoop of ice cream, think about the years of history that went into it and enjoy!

Hey, kids! Now that you're an expert on the history of ice cream, turn the page to learn even more about it and some geography and science along the way!

Ice Cream Around the World

Check out these fascinating flavors we found from different countries all over the world. Which ones sound good to you?

Argentina: *Dulce de leche* Ice Cream — A smooth and tasty dessert that is popular in South America, "*dulce de leche*" means "caramel" in Spanish, and it makes this flavor of ice cream extra sweet.

France: Caviar Ice Cream — In France you can try caviar-flavored ice cream, made with real caviar (otherwise known as fish eggs!).

Germany: Apple Strudel Ice Cream — "Strudel" is a flaky pastry with a creamy flavored filling that is a traditional dessert in Germany. This flavor of ice cream tastes just like it.

Israel: Cardamom Ice Cream — A common ingredient in Middle Eastern recipes, cardamom is a strong spice that gives this ice-cream flavor a kick!

Japan: Squid Ink Ice Cream — A squid is a marine animal similar to an octopus that has a long head and two extra-long tentacles. Squid ink is used in many pasta dishes throughout Asia, but if you travel to Japan you can also try squid ink–flavored ice cream. We hear it tastes salty!

New Zealand: Hokey Pokey Ice Cream — In New Zealand, "Hokey Pokey" ice cream consists of vanilla ice cream with pieces of crunchy honeycomb toffee inside.

Philippines: Cheese Ice Cream — In the Philippines, you'll find chunks of actual cheddar cheese in this savory-sweet ice cream.

Singapore: Chili Pepper Ice Cream — This spicy ice-cream flavor comes from Singapore, where hot chili peppers are blended with a tomato-based ice cream.

Hope you enjoyed this sweet trip around the world! If you could invent your own flavor of ice cream, what would it be?

The Science of Making Ice Cream

Today ice cream is usually made with the big industrial machines used in factories, or the simple countertop ice-cream makers used at home. But as you learned, Nancy Johnson started it all in 1843, when she invented a hand-cranked machine that could churn out ice cream faster than ever before!

Johnson's hand-cranked ice-cream maker used a simple **endothermic reaction** to freeze ice cream. But what is an endothermic reaction?

A **reaction** happens when one thing becomes another. For example, when you leave a can of soda open for too long, it will lose its fizz. This happens because the carbon dioxide (the fizzy bubbles) in soda changes from a liquid to a gas, rises to the top of the soda, and then escapes into the air.

The word **endothermic** is used to describe any process that requires heat. Using heat to melt ice cubes into water is an endothermic process.

So, an **endothermic reaction** is a reaction that requires heat to turn one thing into another. Baking a cake is a great example of an endothermic reaction: A set of ingredients, like flour, sugar, and eggs, plus heat from the oven, react to create a cake.

Now that we know what an endothermic reaction is, let's take a look at a hand-cranked ice-cream maker. These ice-cream makers have three parts: an **outer bucket**, an **inner container**, and a **mixing tool**.

To make ice cream, you pour the ingredients into the inner container, which is then sealed shut with the mixing tool inside. Next you fill the outer bucket with ice and salt, fitting the inner container in the middle of the ice-salt mixture.

When salt mixes with ice, it causes an **endothermic reaction**. The reaction sucks up all of the heat from its surroundings, freezing the ice cream inside the inner container. The salt also lowers the freezing point of the ice, allowing the ice-salt mixture to get as cold as -21° Celsius. That is really cold!

While the **endothermic reaction** takes place, the mixing tool stirs the ice cream inside. As the ice cream is stirred, the liquid ingredients freeze into a creamy solid.

Who knew science could be so delicious?

Fun Fact! Do you know why we pour salt on snowy sidewalks? As we've just seen in our ice-cream maker, salt lowers the freezing point of water. This means that salt both melts the snow on walkways *and* makes it much harder for the water to refreeze unless it gets very, very cold. Presto! No more slippery sidewalks in the winter!

Being an expert on something means you can get an awesome score on a quiz on that subject! Take this

HISTORY OF ICE CREAM QUIZ
to see how much you've learned.

1. Frozen treats have been enjoyed for at least _____ years.

a. 100   b. 450,000   c. 2,000

2. Which emperor ruled the Roman Empire from the year 54 to the year 68 AD?

a. Alexander   b. Nero   c. Augustus

3. The first president of the United States, _____, spent $200 on ice cream in just one summer!

a. George Washington   b. Zachary Taylor   c. Abraham Lincoln

4. Thomas Jefferson discovered a recipe for ice cream while serving as ambassador to which country?

a. Russia   b. France   c. Holland

5. Ice cream wasn't made in factories until what year?

a. 1492   b. 1957   c. 1851

6. The ice-cream cone became popular at the world's fair in _____.

a. Shanghai   b. Alexandria   c. St. Louis

7. When immigrants arrived at _____ in the early 1900s, they were served ice cream.

a. Ellis Island   b. San Francisco   c. Chicago

8. What do Argentina's *dulce de leche* ice cream and Germany's apple strudel ice cream have in common?

a. Both contain squid ink.   b. Both are based on popular desserts.
c. Nothing! They are completely different.

Answers: 1. c 2. b 3. a 4. b 5. c 6. c 7. a 8. b